Dedicated to The Mystery Of Life

This great book of the universe
Galileo
Astronomer

The life-force of the earth is water...
Even in a stone there is this force,
for there is moisture in everything
Ogotemmeli
Dogon Elder

Text copyright © 2003 John Agard
Illustrations copyright © 2003 Satoshi Kitamura

First published in Great Britain in 2003 by Hodder Wayland, an imprint of
Hodder Children's Books

This paperback edition published 2013

A catalogue record for this book is available from the British Library

'Superbugs' Chorus' first performed on BBC TV's 'Newsnight' and printed
in *Bard at the Beeb* by John Agard (BBC Publications, 1998)

ISBN 9781444917727

Printed and bound by CPI Group (UK) Ltd, Croydon, CR0 4YY

Hodder Children's Books
A division of Hodder Headline Limited
338 Euston Road, London NW1 3BH

Hello H2O

Poems by John Agard
Pictures by Satoshi Kitamura

*Hodder
Children's
Books*

A division of Hachette Children's Books

CONTENTS

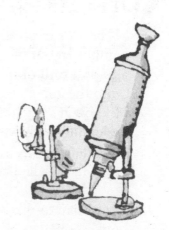

When It's Freezing

When it's freezing
and my mouth
sends a trail of mist
into the air,
I know it's my lungs
releasing water vapour,
clouding up my glasses
by what's called condensation.

But I like to think
my mouth
is an Aladdin's lamp
and from my throat
a genie of smoke
is soaring.

Walking Pendulum

Mood swings.

Now I'm up.

Now I sing.

Now I'm glad.

Mood swings.

Now I'm down.

Now I sulk.

Now I'm glum.

Inertia	and	gravity
must be	turning	me
into a	walking	pendulum.

Hello H2O

Your body
is an ocean's body,
your skin
is a river's skin.

In your footsteps
the rain dances,
in your shadow
a lake sees itself.

With your echo
a waterfall speaks,
with your gestures
a fountain splashes itself.

You leave your signature
in puddles and leaks
– each a small reminder
that water was here.

Hello H2O,
my two parts hydrogen,
one part oxygen friend
from my womb-swimming past.

My mouth will always be your glass.

My Humanoid Robot

My humanoid robot
has a brain that's powered
by a dual pentium
3 processor.

My humanoid robot
has gauges and sensors
all nicely built-in
to give it softer skin.

My humanoid robot
is an early riser,
no sleepyhead dosser,
and wakes me every morning.

My humanoid robot
helps to keep my room neat
and can easily beat
Dad at a game of Chess.

Still, Mum isn't impressed.
Whenever they compete,
she calls my humanoid robot
'a clever little cheat.'

Then my humanoid robot
flies off its pentium
and throws such a tantrum,
you'd swear it was human.

To you
I'm blowing bubbles.
To me
I'm conducting
an orchestra
of swirling light waves
and rainbow octaves.

To you
I'm blowing bubbles.
To me
I'm building
a nest
of planets
on a branch of breath.

It's Sad When A Kite's

forward motion
to the sky
becomes a backward
motion to the ground –
a colourful ruin
at your feet.

Your flying dragon
now fully earthbound.
Your singing bird
has lost its tongue.
Your dancing fish
collapsed in a heap.

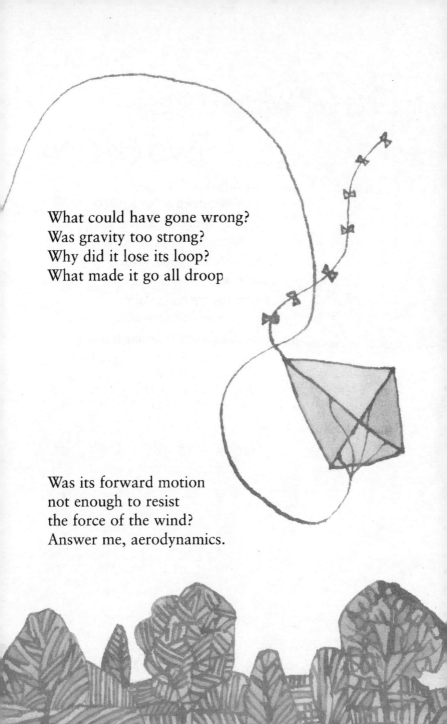

What could have gone wrong?
Was gravity too strong?
Why did it lose its loop?
What made it go all droop

Was its forward motion
not enough to resist
the force of the wind?
Answer me, aerodynamics.

Two Of One

Little Bo Peep
has lost her cloned sheep
but she isn't
the least bit bothered,
for wherever one roams
there roams the other.
So she leaves them alone,
knowing they'll come home,
bringing each other's chromosomes.

But what would Little Bo Peep do,
if she were to meet
under a haycock fast asleep,
not one but two
of Little Boy Blue?
Each one an exact copy
of the other,
and each one just as lazy
as the other.

Neither blowing his horn
Neither blowing his horn

No thought
for the sheep in the meadow
No thought
for the cow in the corn.

A Watt?

You ask me
what's a watt?
Better ask Mr. Watt.
He'll tell you what's what
on the subject of watts.
He comes from a long line of Watts.
All I know
is that a watt's
got something
to do with a lightbulb's glow.
That's what,
or whatever.

The Bald Man's Reply

What would a bald man
want with a comb?
When I rub this comb
along the atomic
particles
of my shiny
egg of a head,
and the teeth tickle
my knackered
follicles,
I remind myself
how once my hair
was elastic.
And believe you me,
my skull begins to glow
with the mere memory
of static.

It's Shining Watermelons

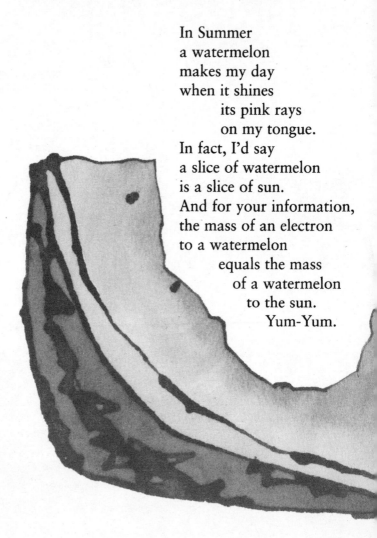

In Summer
a watermelon
makes my day
when it shines
    its pink rays
    on my tongue.
In fact, I'd say
a slice of watermelon
is a slice of sun.
And for your information,
the mass of an electron
to a watermelon
    equals the mass
      of a watermelon
    to the sun.
        Yum-Yum.

Recipe For A Floating Chinese Compass

Take a thin leaf of iron.
Marinate with a lodestone.
Flatten into shape of fish.
Heat until red hot.
Remove from fire with tongs.
Float in a bowl of seawater.
Head of fish will point south.
Tail of fish will point true north.
Say long live magnetised needle.

Clockwise

I'm your bedside mate.
And I'll let you all
into a secret.
If my quartz crystal
didn't oscillate
to tune my pulse rate
to ticking tempo,
you'll surely be late.

But I say nothing.
Just sit in my place
as squat as a toad
and keep a straight face,
pointing to time's road.
Tomorrow at dawn,
I'm set to alarm.
May your dreams be deep
when I steal your sleep.

Melting Point

'Why are you crying?'
the little girl asked the giant.

'Because solids melt
at a certain temperature,'
the giant replied.

The little girl nodded, 'that's right.
Plutonium, for example, has a melting point
of 1184 degrees Fahrenheit.'

The giant sighed and said, 'you're very bright.
And it seems I've just met my melting point.'

With that, the giant cried
himself into a fountain.

Speculating About Specs

'Let us give thanks
for convex lenses,'
said the long-sighted.

'Let us give thanks
for concave lenses,'
said the short-sighted.

'Let us give thanks
for noses,' said the clown.
'Of course, I'm delighted

with my new pair of specs.
But if noses didn't exist,
how would we balance these discs?'

A Few Questions For The Tooth Fairy

I have a few questions
for the tooth fairy.
Now, don't get me wrong,
I certainly welcome
waking to a coin
under my pillow.
But I need to know
the truth, the whole truth
and nothing but the truth.
What would a fairy want
with a once wobbly tooth?
Does she recycle it?
Can it be that tooth fairies
eat too may sweets?
Do they get rotten teeth?

Do they have cavities
that need to be filled?
Have they their own kind
of dental drill
and ultra-sound probe
to help them fight plaque?
Is there fluoride
in fairy drinking water
or do they just fly off
to calcium-rich flowery places?
These are a few of the questions
I'm dying to ask.
And I'd do anything
to see a tooth fairy
smiling with braces.

Five Reasons Why I Would Volunteer For Outer Space

1. It would be good to live in a weightless neighbourhood.

2. I could do my homework while turning somersaults.

3. It would be fun
   to watch my spoon
   fly away
   from my Cocoa Pops.

4. I could boast
   I've actually been
   to the loo
   on the moon.

5. If I'm late
   I could say
   'My alarm clock, Miss,
   Just floated off.'

The Day The Metals Marched

Out of the earth's crust they come.
Out of the furnace they come
after centuries of combustion.
From every direction they come
and they need no drum –
these molten messengers
marching, marching to the sound
of their own names:

Aurum
Argentum
Cuprum
Ferrum
Staunum

All taking up position.
All ready to stand as one,
despite their different forms
of lumps, blades, jewels, wires, rods.
All in blinding splendour.
Iron and Bronze rubbing shoulders.
Gold and Silver mingling rays.
Copper glinting next to Tin –

And on the day the metals marched
Plumbum just couldn't wait to join in.
Yes, old Plumbum, better known as Lead,
though grey of hair and slow of foot,
fell in line with –

> Aurum
> Argentum
> Cuprum
> Ferrum
> Staunum

Meanwhile, the humans stayed indoors.

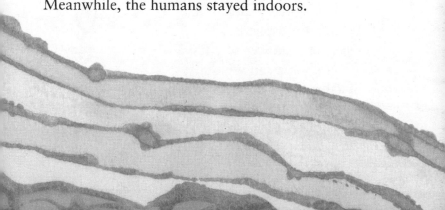

Gifts For Earth's Atmosphere

By sea, by land, by air
they came bearing gifts
to Earth's atmosphere.

Nitrogen and Oxygen
were most generous
with their own gases.
And Argon and Carbon Dioxide
also took pride
in giving themselves.

And water brought vapour
and crystals of ice,
and the ocean thought
a bouquet of salt
would be nice,
and the flowers
not to be outdone,
presented their pollen
in wind-wrapped particles.

And from every direction,
Earth's atmosphere
received a shower of gifts
– including a sad windfall
of ashes and soot
and gases that pollute.

Atmospheric Traveller

Of course, I've braved
the six layers
of the atmosphere.
You name it, I've been there.

From the dense Troposphere
to the less dense Stratosphere,
through a chemical buzz
of the Mesosphere,
past the plasma
of the Ionosphere,
rising higher
to the raging Thermosphere,
till I came at last
to the Exosphere,
where weird gases
made me welcome.

But I'd rather
settle down here
among common
stones and grasses.
Other spheres
are not for me,
I feel safer
with gravity.

Pigeon's Flying Tips

'It's all to do with lift and thrust,'
said the pigeon to the pilot.
'I lift my wings at take-off time.
And in the wind I place my trust.
By the way, my propeller
never needs to be replaced.
And all the sky's my airspace.'

Leonardo da Vinci's Notebooks

To Leonardo da Vinci,
a bird in flight
was an aerodynamic delight.

What better way to learn
about aerial locomotion
than from creatures born for aviation?

So he studied birds, sketched birds –
their lift, their glide, their wing movements.
He even studied wind currents.

Then he turned his thoughts
from the miracle of feathers
to ordinary things like propellers.

And four hundred years or more,
before a helicopter was seen,
he designed a flying machine.

They called it Ornithopter,
a funny sort of word
that comes from the Greek for bird.

This isn't surprising.
And he must have had fun jotting down
forward ideas in backwards handwriting.

Strictly Speaking

Strictly speaking, they say
the moon doesn't shine
since it has no light
of its own.
Strictly speaking, they say
the moon's glow
is a sun-loan.

But on a full-moon night
when stars flock that yellow,
it's no business of mine
if the moon does borrow
the sun's light.
When it's dark
I borrow from the moon.

Daydreaming Galileo

'Daydreaming again, Galileo?'
his teacher asked with a frown.
'Aren't you supposed to be reading?'

'I am,' replied Galileo.
'Don't you see my eyes turning
the pages of the skies?

I'm busy browsing
the grand book of the universe.
A book I simply can't put down.'

Under Galileo's Glass

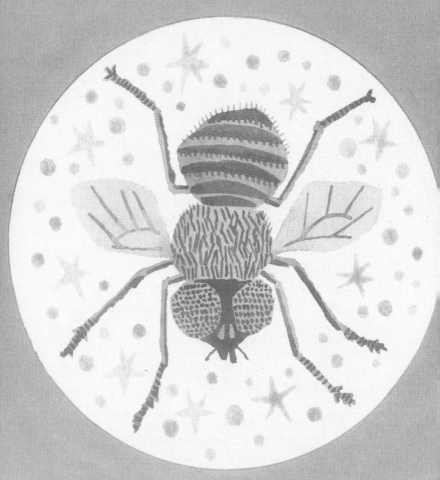

A tiny gnat
shows off its godliness.

A grey moth
becomes a galaxy.

An upside down fly
puts on the wings of a star.

And is that a horrible
bloodsucking flea

treating the eye
to a small constellation?

All this is possible
under Galileo's glass.

Even the smallest
of creepy-crawlies

dares you to guess
its wriggling zodiac.

One Family?

If I am made
of atoms and molecules,
and you are made
of atoms and molecules,
and all the world is made
of atoms and molecules,
does this mean the human race
belongs to one family
of atoms and molecules?
Then why aren't we as together
as tadpoles in a pool?
They never teach you this
in science at school.

Weighty Thoughts

Isn't it great,
thought the astronaut,
to be free
of gravity –
a dangling bait
in a weightless sea.

One thing bothers me,
thought the astronaut.
If my spaceship lands
at heaven's gate,
will my earthly words
still bear weight?

And Then The Sun Spoke

Take all the fuel
known to planet earth.

Burn your wood, your coal,
get your oil roaring.

The energy soaring
from your humble fires

will be nowhere near
a billionth –

Yes, a billionth
of the heat and light

I provide for free.
And the trees thank me

for my radiance.
And the flowers flutter

their appreciation.
And how do the humans

acknowledge Sun's favours?
Believe it or not –

By sunshades and sunblock.

DNA(1)

It's easier
to say
DNA –
that's no tongue twister.

But somehow
I feel a whizz kid
when I say
DEOXYRIBONUCLEIC ACID

especially
with my mouth full.

DNA(2)

Adenine: Guanine
Cytosine: Thymine.
They come in pairs
and they're all yours,
all mine.

Building blocks we share
with living things.
Whether curled
within a nucleus
or floating free,
they make us us,
unique you,
unique me.

DNA (3)

If I climb
the ladder
of my DNA
would I lose my way
among the cells
of my body?

Would it be okay to step on
those chemical rungs
and balance
on spiralling pairs
of nitrogen bases?
What awaits
among those sugars
and phosphates?

Would they lead me
to magic places
and marvels of mind
or would I find
myself
face to face
with skeletons
in a cupboard?

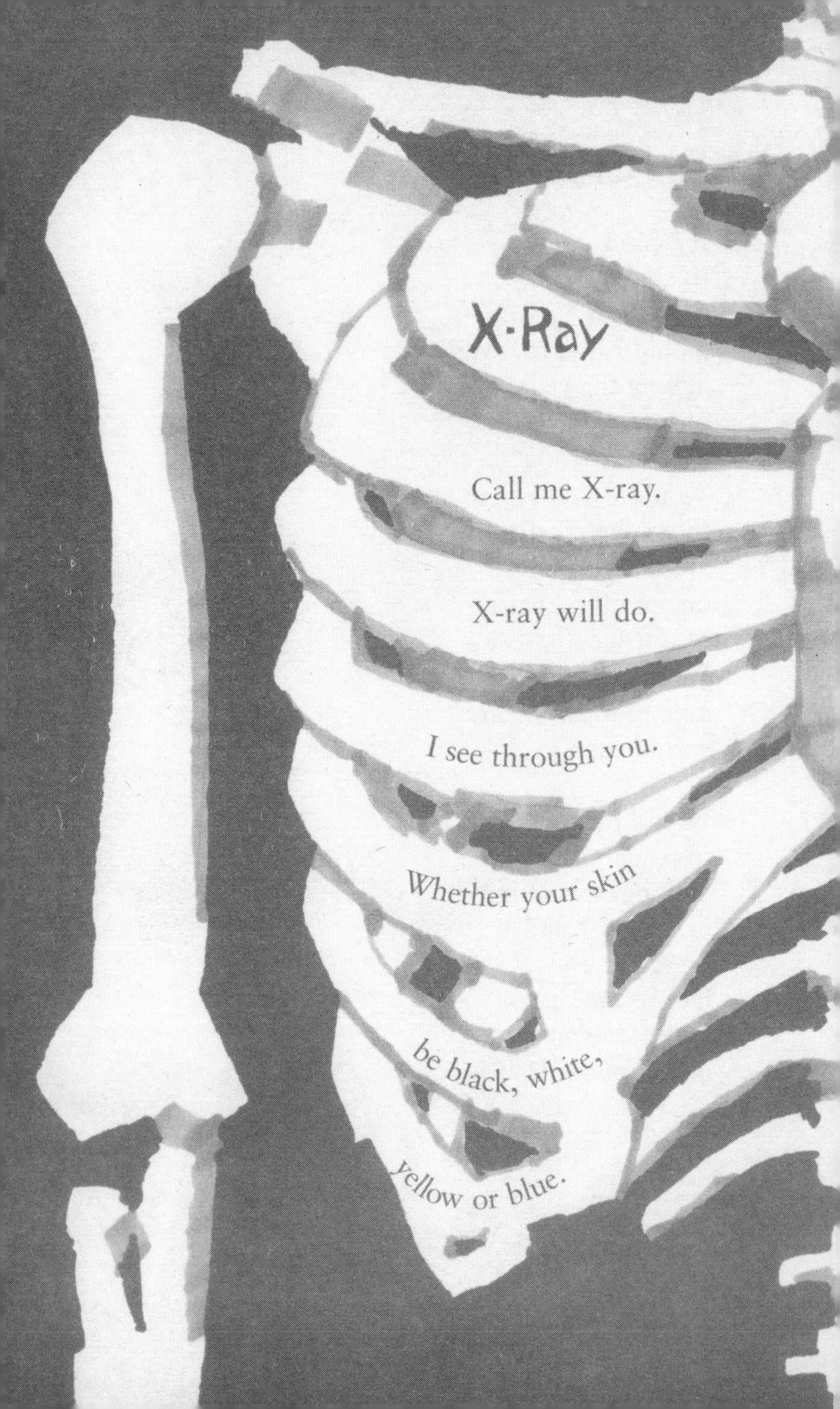

X-Ray

Call me X-ray.

X-ray will do.

I see through you.

Whether your skin

be black, white,

yellow or blue.

An inside view

is what I get.

That's a fact, mate.

I offer you

your skeleton

served on a photographic

plate.

The Wind Sets The Record Right

'It's not electricity
making those telephone wires hum.

It's my velocity.
Yes, it's me, it's me,' said the wind.

'It's the plectrum
of my breath
as I strum
those telephone wires
for my guitar.

I the wind
serenading
a star.'

Cloud Chant

You call us
names like 'ominous'
but we call our grey 'glorious'

I thundery Cumulonimbus
I showery Nimbostratus
I crystally Cirrostratus
I drizzly Stratocumulus
I icy Cirrocumulus
I watery Altocumulus

Feathery we may be
Foggy we may be
Woolly we may be
Wispy we may be

But grand is our status –
we grand descendants
of Cumulus, Cirrus and Stratus.

Photosynthesis

When sunlight dances
on the tips
of leaves

and plants for joy
open their lips
to drink it in

and the breeze
makes a violin
of every tree

and even weeds
one by one
cry out for a kiss

of light and carbon –
a sheer spree of green.
Is this what they mean

by photosynthesis?

Consider The Peanut

Consider the peanut,
this humble jewel
housed in a shell.
Consider the peanut,
this small traveller
across continents
with many secrets to tell.

Consider the peanut,
and consider
George Washington Carver
and his peanut experiments.
From peanuts and their skins and shells,
he brought forth diesel fuel,
writing ink, newsprint paper,
not to mention face ointments,
toilet soap, toothpaste, shampoo,
even shoe polish,
and of course peanut dainties
like brownies and caramel.

Consider the peanut,
and consider
this plant doctor
who learnt to read, write and spell,
even as he saw his parents wake
to slavery's bell
and heard the music of the blues.
He would make the peanut story
his life's study
for his 'cookstove chemistry.'
Yes, he would spread the good news
of the unsung peanut –

this winged bean
that ripens underground,
this lifeline vine
for forest-dwellers,
this decoration
on an Inca pot,
this discovery
in an Egyptian tomb,
and in years to come –
this astronaut's gift
from planet earth to moon.

We, The Noble Gases

We, the noble gases,
are the upper classes
of the atmosphere.
When we throw a party,
it's a very private affair.
Strictly by invitation
and liquid distillation.
We don't easily mix, we six.

Can Lord and Lady Argon,
Krypton, Neon, Xenon, Radon,
not to mention
His Highness Helium,
rub shoulders with the common?
We, the noble gases,
maintain our noble station
in noble isolation.

The Dead Sea Speaks

Freshwater streams may feed me,
yet salt is my destiny
and brine my very being.

People talk a lot
about my deadly salinity,
my density, my whatnot.

But from the depths of my valleybed
across the burning desert sands,
let these words of mine flow red.

Dead Sea I am in name, but not in deed,
for underneath my salty shroud
countless living microbes do me proud.

Superbugs' Chorus

Superbugs, that's us, anonymous.
Germs. Microbes. Bacillus.
Come on folks, what's all the fuss?
Join the bacteria chorus.
We invisible hordes
colonise your chopping boards,
squat upon your rugs,
reside within your hair,
lay down roots everywhere,
for we are superbugs.
Send in the penicillin.
Bring on the ampicillin.

We'll have a lie-in in your skin.
So consider yourself immune
all smug in your germ-free cocoon?
We'll catch you and catch you soon.
You there in your squeaky-clean zone,
we're nesting in your mobile phone.
Yet we superbugs are rays of hope,
we bring life to your microscope.
So why not give decay a chance
and share the planet with our kind?
We are the children of your waste,
the offspring of your extravagance,
and while humans dine and die,
we superbugs dance, we dance.

Who'll Save Dying Man?

Who'll save dying Man?
  I, said the Baboon.
Transplant my bone marrow,
and he'll wake tomorrow.

Who'll save dying Man?
  I, said the Chimpanzee.
He's welcome to my brain,
for deep down we're the same.

Who'll save dying Man?
  I, said the Pig.
I'll give him my liver.
May he live forever.

Who'll save dying Man?
  I, said the Sheep.
Let him have my kidney,
and that would be for free.

Who'll save dying Man?
  I, said Rat.
My retina would do
to make his vision new.

Who'll save dying Man?
   I, said Squid.
He can have our nerve cells,
for sea-folk wish him well.

Who'll save dying Man?
   I, said the Physician.
I'll save him with my skills,
though dying Man once killed.

Thanks for the offer,
   said dying Man.
But I'd like to request
a Dodo for a doner.

And the animals fell
a-whispering secretly:
   O dying Man
has lost his memory.

Radium And Madame Curie

The birds didn't sing,
the bees didn't hum,
when Marie Curie
discovered Radium.

But the atoms danced
their secret dance,
happy to release
their energy.

Marie had worked for years
with her husband Pierre,
and to the Curies,
physics was their chemistry.

Marie would leave her bed
for her drafty shed,
drawn to the mystery
of a new element.

She had to explore
this unnamed continent –
map out the rays
that turned air to glow-worms.

And with no protective clothing,
she dared to greet Radium
– great healer
– great destroyer.

That's why the birds didn't sing
and the bees didn't hum.
But the nuclear atoms
danced to their own drum.

In Praise of The Eraser

I would not chew
on the delete key
of the computer
if I were you.

So sing in praise
of the eraser,
your little chewy
vulcanised buddy.

Someone once said,
'any fool can write.
It takes a genius
to erase.'

Now at my PC
lost in thought's deep mist,
I must say I miss
an eraser's kiss.

To erase is bliss.

Electro·Magnetic Haunting

Since an electro-magnetic wave passes
through solids, liquids and gases
and invisibly enters a room,

it would be great to come back from the grave
as an electro-magnetic wave.
On Halloween night, I'd haunt a vacuum.

Quivers In The Life Of A Quark

1.
A Quark
can neither
quack not bark

for a Quark
is neither
duck nor dog

though perhaps
a bit of both.
A Quark

likes to swim
in a cosmic tub
as it wags

its tail
in the sub-
atomic

dark.

2.
An atom called Quark
met an atom called Anti-Quark.

But neither knew
what the other was called,
and it didn't matter.
A Quark to a Quark was a Quark,
whether red, green or blue.

Without any fuss,
Quark and Anti-Quark
quivered their particles
on a cosmic ray.

And to this day
Quark and Anti-Quark
live in a nucleus

And their sub-atomic marriage
remains a mystery to us.

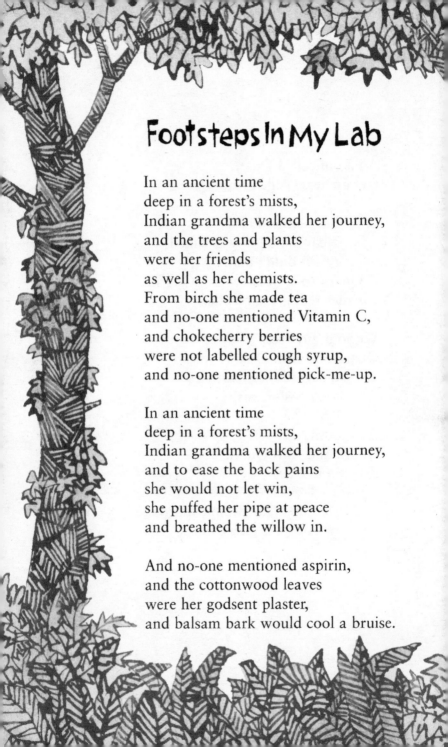

Footsteps In My Lab

In an ancient time
deep in a forest's mists,
Indian grandma walked her journey,
and the trees and plants
were her friends
as well as her chemists.
From birch she made tea
and no-one mentioned Vitamin C,
and chokecherry berries
were not labelled cough syrup,
and no-one mentioned pick-me-up.

In an ancient time
deep in a forest's mists,
Indian grandma walked her journey,
and to ease the back pains
she would not let win,
she puffed her pipe at peace
and breathed the willow in.

And no-one mentioned aspirin,
and the cottonwood leaves
were her godsent plaster,
and balsam bark would cool a bruise.

In an ancient time
deep in a forest's mists,
Indian grandma walked her journey,
and to stop a fever
beating its sweating drum
on a grandchild's brow,
she would ask the help
of wild geranium.
And raspberry was ready
for a runny tummy,
and no-one mentioned prescription.

Indian grandma, long gone to rest.
Your medicine bag
still haunts my medicine chest.
I hear your footsteps in my lab.

NOTES

p. 24 Two thousand years ago, the Chinese were already experimenting with compasses, first using a lodestone carved in the shape of a ladle. Later they used a magnetised needle and the 'south-pointing fish' made from a flat leaf of iron. It was the Arabs who introduced the Chinese idea to the Western world. Without this method of 'navigating by needle', many European voyages would not have been possible.

p. 18 In the plant world, a lot of 'cloning' goes on. A twig that is planted in the ground, or grafted to the branch of another tree, is known as a 'clone' from the Greek word for twig. In July 1996 a sheep was scientifically reproduced in this manner. Dolly, the world's first cloned mammal, was born. Dolly went on to have six lambs and died in February 2003. The debate continues whether it is right or not to clone mammals.

p. 40 Leonardo da Vinci was born in 1452 in Vinci, Italy. He not only played the lute and painted the famous Mona Lisa. He also spent days dissecting bodies to discover the secrets of anatomy. After his death in 1519, he left behind thousands of pages of notebooks, filled with sketches and ideas for inventions, some of them even looking like modern-day helicopters and scuba diving equipment. But you'll need a mirror to read his notebooks, for Leonardo wrote in mirror-writing.

p. 46 Galileo was born in 1564 in Pisa, Italy. Apparently, he wasn't too keen on science at school but he grew up to be a legendary sky-watcher. He also used his telescope as a microscope and was fascinated to see 'flies which look as big as lambs'. Even when he became blind in 1637, he was still making discoveries in astronomy. He was persecuted for his belief that the earth went around the sun. He died at the age of seventy-eight, knowing that he was right.

p. 52 D.N.A, or deoxyribonucleic acid if you prefer, has been described as a sort of alphabet we inherit in a molecule that stores information that makes us who we are. This D.N.A molecule connects us to our furthest ancestors and its shape has been compared to a ladder or two coiled together snakes. Among peoples such as the Aborigines and the Amazonian Indians, there is a belief that ancestral spirits descend a ladder and that all creation was the work of a 'cosmic serpent.'

p. 62 George Washington Carver was born around 1865 in Missouri, U.S.A. during the time of slavery. As a boy, he was always curious about plants, and went on to be the first African-American member of the faculty at Iowa State College. As an agricultural scientist, or 'plant doctor', he was best known for his experiments with peanuts, using them for soil improvement and even for household items like soap and shoe polish. His face appeared on a stamp and a coin. The farm that was his birthplace is a national monument. He died in 1943.

p. 70 Physicist Madame Curie was born Marya Sklodowska in Poland in 1867. She won two Nobel Prizes for both Physics and Chemistry – one in 1903 shared with her Chemist husband, Pierre Curie, and one in 1911 for her discovery of polonium and radium. When she first saw Radium in the shed she used as a laboratory, she said 'it was really a lovely sight and always new to us. The glowing tubes looked like faint fairy lights.' But this luminous element is also known to have harmful effects. Marie died in 1934 of an aplastic anemica, a sickness which is believed to be the result of handling radium without protection.

p. 74 Any queries about Quarks, especially quirky queries, are best addressed to Quarks themselves. But you'll have to travel to the very centre of a nucleus to meet these shifty particles that came to the attention of scientists in the 1960s.

p. 76 For American Indians, plants possessed a living spirit and were nature's healers. The Indians knew that the willow was a good painkiller long before western science discovered it as the 'aspirin tree.'

Among the books which have been beacons in a sea of facts as well as wonder, I owe my thanks to:

Isaac Asimov's *New guide To Science* (Penguin); Peter James and Nick Thorpe's *Ancient Inventions* (Michael O'Mara Books Limited); Marcel Griaule's *Conversations With Ogotmmeli*; (Oxford University Press); David Peat's *Blackfoot Physics* (Fourth Estate); Lisa Yount's *Black Scientists* (Facts on File Inc.); Dava Sobel's *Galileo's Daughter* (Fourth Estate); Oliver Sacks' *Uncle Tungsten* (Picador); Frances Ashcroft's *Life At The Extremes* (Flamingo); Jeremy Narby's *The Cosmic Serpent* (Pheonix)

And my thanks to the Hodder Team and as ever to Satoshi Kitamura.